Hugh Barclay

TENNIS

TENNIS

BY

PANCHO GONZALES

AND

DICK HAWK

Edited by
GLADYS HELDMAN
World Tennis Magazine

AVENEL BOOKS • NEW YORK

DEDICATION

To the youth of America—
in an endeavor to help them
achieve happiness in a noble
way of life through a clean,
healthy, wholesome activity.
—PANCHO GONZALES

The publisher wishes to acknowledge the invaluable assistance rendered by the following in the preparation and planning of this book:
Mr. Ted Patrick, Editor of *Holiday Magazine*; Mr. Ed. Thomas of Abercrombie & Fitch; Mr. Charles Wilbur of A. G. Spalding Corp.; Mr. Edwin Baker, Executive Secretary, U. S. Lawn Tennis Association; and Mr. Bryan Hamlin of Bridgehampton, N.Y.

FOREWORD

In my years as an instructor of tennis, I have often felt the need for a really first-rate book on the essentials of tennis. The few books on the market today are too long and tend to confuse the tennis player, seeking only to improve his game, with intricate discussions of strategy and little-used shots.

I asked myself who would be the tennis player best qualified to write a book which would aim only at improving the game of novice and expert alike. The name that immediately came to my mind was that of Pancho Gonzales, the world's greatest tennis player.

Here, then, is a book designed to be used *on the court,* a complete tennis manual written by the sport's finest natural champion. Pancho Gonzales explains the correct grip and stroke for every shot in a manner that leaves no room for confusion. Study the book at home first, then take it *on the court* and, with a friend, take a lesson from the master. You will be amazed at the rapid improvement in your game.

—DICK HAWK

CONTENTS

INTRODUCTION

Pancho Gonzales is the most natural player who ever lived. He never had a formal tennis lesson, and yet his strokes are classical. He had almost no tournament competition during his formative years, but he was an outstanding player at the age of 19. At that time he played his first big event, which was the Southern California Championships. He defeated 19-year-old Herb Flam, who was the current National Junior Champion. This was the first in a long series of big tournament wins.

Richard Alonzo Gonzales, better known as Pancho, was born in Los Angeles on May 9, 1928. He was one of seven children. Although he was raised in the depression years, the Gonzales family never knew real poverty. There was plenty of food, and clean clothes, but few luxuries. Pancho says that when he was a little boy, he liked to eat beans, milk, oatmeal, salad and tortillas. Today he still likes to eat them! He did not drink coffee until he was 17, and he never smoked until he went into the Navy. He takes an occasional drink, but he does everything in moderation. He is a perfect example of a physically fit athlete who, in his early thirties, is in better condition than most players 10 years his junior.

After Pancho beat Herb Flam, he decided to compete in the big Eastern tournaments. He was inexperienced, and both clay and grass courts were new to him; he had played only on cement. Nevertheless, he managed to earn a No. 17 ranking when the national lists were posted. The following year (1948), he again played the Eastern tennis circuit. This time he was unbeatable. He won the U.S. National Championships at Forest Hills, beating Eric Sturgess of South Africa in the final round. He was just 20, and he was ranked No. 1 in the country. The next year he again won the national title, this time beating the formidable Ted Schroeder. He then decided to turn professional.

11

Pancho was the best amateur in the world, but he was not yet the best professional. He was decisively beaten by top pro Jack Kramer in a series of exhibitions throughout the country. The professionals in those days played tours rather than tournaments. The No. 1 pro regularly took on the No. 1 amateur from the previous year. The winner stayed on to play the tour the following year, but the loser was out. Pancho's loss to Kramer put him on the sidelines. Despite his eagerness, it was *five years* before he was back on the pro tour again. From here on, he was the World Champion. In the tours that followed, he beat Tony Trabert, Frank Sedgman, Pancho Segura, Ken Rosewall, Lew Hoad, Alex Olmedo, Butch Buchholz, and Barry MacKay. At the end of the 1961 tour, he announced his retirement from competition. He had proved himself one of the greatest players of all time.

The Gonzales game has been admired by every top player. He has no critics. He is universally recognized as a great stylist, a hungry competitor and a winner. It is a tennis aphorism that it is far easier to become a world champion than it is to stay at the top. Once a player has reached the pinnacle, he can suffer from fear of losing or he can lose his hunger for winning. Pancho was always courageous, and success never softened him. He is as hard today as he was when he was struggling for recognition back in 1947. He is as tough a competitor as the world has ever known. He gives no quarter, and the old venom that made him become a winner is still the most significant characteristic of his court personality. He is a tennis killer in the best sense of the word.

Gonzales has a great temperament for the game. Despite the fact that his attack seems to be motivated by sullen, cold fury or murderous determination, his inner turmoil has never caused him to lose a match. He can play badly and be beaten, or on a given day he can be trounced by a colossus such as Lew Hoad, but his temperamental displays have never affected his own game. If he is licked by Hoad on a Monday, he is more than liable to reverse the score on Tuesday. Losing has the effect of stirring him up, and when he starts winning he is never headed.

The Gonzales game has nothing but virtues. Every stroke is beautifully executed, he plays with consummate grace, and he never makes the wrong shot. He makes tennis look too easy. Gonzales has always been known as a great attacker, but he is equally as great in the role of defensive player. Everyone acknowledges the magnificence of his service, volleying and overheads, but he is equally strong in lobbing, running down balls and nailing placements on passing shots. Pancho Segura once said that Gonzales was the only big man who attacked who could also defend well. There is no hint of clumsiness in his game. He covers a prodigious amount of court with so little effort that few spectators realize how well he retrieves.

The Serve

The Gonzales service is a natural action that epitomizes grace, power, control and placement. The top players sigh when they see the smooth, easy action. There is no trace of a hitch, and no extra furbelows. I have never seen a serve so beautifully executed. The toss is no higher than it has to be, and it is timed so that he is fully stretched when he hits it. The backswing is continuous; the motion of the backswing blends into the hit and continues into the follow-through without a pause.

Pancho is not a heavy spin server. His first serve is almost flat, and the second has a modicum of slice or roll. Slice is produced by moving the racket face across the ball from left to right; American twist is given to the ball by moving the racket face from left to right and over the ball with a pronounced wrist snap—the ball is halfway between the slice and twist and gives the ball forward spin rather than spin to the left or right. The slice or roll that Gonzales gives to the ball is just enough for control on second serve. The slice serve gives more forward thrust than the American twist, and also makes it possible to serve the ball deeper in the service court.

13

The strongest part of Gonzales' serve is his ability to put his first service into play when the chips are down. At 0-40, 15-40 and 30-40, his batting average on first serves must be .950. It is incredible to have so high a percentage while still hitting hard and almost flat. The number of aces served on these important points is also astounding. No other player has been able to perform this feat so regularly.

The Overhead

Pancho is not a leaper on the overhead, and he does not have that wristy, flat snap that bounces them very high. He hits the ball with a little spin in a motion that is almost identical with his serve. He literally pole-axes the overhead just as he punishes the serve. Gonzales seems to have an infallible sense of where to hit the ball; more than any other player, he catches his opponent going the wrong way. Bobby Riggs was deceptive, too, and so is Pancho Segura, but Gonzales has the edge of size.

The Volley

Pancho is a natural net player because of his anticipation and great coordination. He is not particularly a hard volleyer, except for high forehands, which he tends to stroke as do so many of the top players. He has excellent control over sharp angle shots, which he hits rather than "dumps." Most players will use a very small action in "dumping" an angle shot, but Gonzales actually punches the ball to make his angle volley. He plays extremely close to the net except, of course, when he is coming in behind service for the first volley. Standing this far in is dangerous, but gives Gonzales an almost sure winner if he can touch the ball. He chooses mostly angle shots, and only volleys deep on the first ball when he is caught behind the service line. Only a player with great height, reach and anticipation can use this type of tactics, since a lesser man would be lobbed unmercifully.

14

Both the forehand and backhand volley are characterized by underspin. Consistency in the volley is the mark of a top pro in today's game, since the leading players literally camp on the net. Gonzales is consistent in his first volleys, which he plays deep, and in his angle volleys, which he hits sharply.

In the old days, the half-volley was a trick shot used by a player caught in "no man's land." Today it is standard equipment and is used regularly by the server in his approach to net. Gonzales on the forehand side will take a rather full swing on the half-volley. On the backhand, he prefers to take a backward step so that the ball will rise off the ground. Then he uses heavy underspin, preferably crosscourt, and closes in on the net. He uses this technique so frequently that it is an integral part of his style.

The Forehand

Pancho's forehand is not grooved in a distinctive pattern; he will hit with closed or open stance, with a big backswing or none at all, and with a high or low follow-through. Only when he stays back does his forehand take on a grooved look. The backswing is lengthened, and the follow-through definitely shows overspin. If you give him any short ball, he is completely unpredictable. He may shove it from the hip down the line, or leisurely come over it for the crosscourt, or snap his wrist to hit the desired spot on the court. He will block, chip or stroke on return of serve, hitting with all his might when he so desires. Mostly, he will chip against the big serves since he is a "percentage" player and feels the odds are with the chip in keeping the ball in play. On passing shots, he is not afraid to strike out very hard. He is flat and sharp and accurate. This is surprising, since it comes in such contrast to his chip return of serve. He finds that the chip return of service tires the opponent in long matches.

15

Gonzales can hit the backhand in any of the three classical modes: with underspin, flat, or with overspin. He prefers the underspin, but will use one of the other two on passing shots. His flat backhand is extremely powerful, particularly when he is run out of court. The underspin is used on return of serve, which is usually a low crosscourt in the left court. This is his chosen gambit to slow down the game momentarily and to make the opponent volley to his forehand.

His control on the backhand is excellent. It is as smooth as silk and well-grooved. He generally slices when he comes in, but he will vary his backhands when he stays in the backcourt. Most people never appreciated the soundness of his ground game, but the pro tour featuring the three-bounce rule permitted Pancho to demonstrate his all-around competence. He could handle such great ground strokers as Segura or Rosewall from the baseline!

For a decade, players have argued the relative merits of Bill Tilden and Don Budge when discussing the never-ending question of the greatest player of all time. Budge himself now feels that Gonzales has earned the No. 1 spot. The players will never agree on an answer, but the general consensus among top players is a three-way split among Tilden, Budge, and Gonzales.

—Gladys Heldman

16

TENNIS

by

PANCHO GONZALES

1. STRATEGY

Too many players on all levels are unrealistic about their own games. Before working out an elaborate tactical plan relative to your opponent's game, analyze *your own* game in order to cover up or correct weaknesses and to display your full strength.

Your service usually determines whether you will win or lose the match. You may be overhitting your first service every time, or perhaps you are merely trying to put the ball in play. In either case, the error is fatal. Cut down on your power if your first serve is not going in at least 70% of the time. Three or four aces per set are not enough to counterbalance an erratic first delivery. Similarly, a soft or "push" service offers no problems to the opponent. Make a conscious effort to put more sting on the ball. Put your wrist, shoulder and entire body weight into the serve *every time you hit it*.

The return of service is the second most important stroke of the game. If you cannot return your opponent's serve, or if you return it weakly, you will lose every other game. If his serve is hard, try to get ready fast. Watch the ball come off his racket. Don't wait until the ball crosses the net to make your move. If you are having trouble with his spin serve, try standing in one to three feet closer. The sooner you take it after it bounces, the less chance the spin has to be effective. Perhaps you are overhitting on returns. There is no need to skim the net if your opponent is staying back. If he comes in, throw up a few high lobs over his *backhand* side. This will have the effect of keeping him from coming in too close, and your passing shots will then be more effective.

Almost every player is stronger on one side than the other. If your backhand is your weakness, play to the left of the center line. Just how far left you stand depends on your court-covering ability and the pace with which your opponent hits.

Play aggressively on your strong side, but never be trapped into overhitting on your weakness. A smart opponent will try to force you onto your bad side. The correct parry depends upon his court position. If he stays back, simply hit your return *deep* to his weakness; if he comes to net, don't be ashamed to lob as much as you drive; and if his shot is not strong, step around and take it on your stronger side.

Do not try to practice a deficient stroke during a match. In competition, you are trying to make the best possible use of your current stroke equipment. The backboard or hitting sessions are the best times in which to practice, but in match play you must use what you have to best possible advantage.

Placement on overheads and volleys is far more important than pace. You can tell quickly if you are overhitting; there will be too many errors. Shorten your swing to avoid wild slashes at the ball and play your shots more cautiously. Sometimes you may hit too softly. If your opponent is out of position and still can get to your overhead or volley, you are "pushing" the ball instead of punching it. Don't take a bigger stroke, but use your body weight instead to give added pace to the shot.

Common Tactical Errors

If your opponent hits a wide, short ball to your forehand, never return it crosscourt. You have left your whole backhand court open. You either must return down the line and come to net, playing to the right of the center service line, *or* hit a deep ball to the center of your opponent's baseline in order to give you time to get back into position.

If your opponent is on his service line and has dropshotted, never dropshot in return. He is so close-in that he will be on top of the ball. Unless you have a perfectly disguised and beautifully executed dropshot, never use it except when you are inside your service line and your opponent is on his baseline.

Don't hit every ball the same way. If you understand under-spin on the backhand and heavy topspin on the forehand, vary them with your regular drives. However, never use spins if they make your ball fall short. Hit an occasional ball harder than usual and an occasional ball higher or softer (as long as they are deep) than you normally do. Keep your opponent off balance with the unexpected, but do not try shots that are not in your repertoire in a match.

Don't hit every ball to your opponent's weakness. When you get the opening, hit a wide ball to his strength. If your opponent hits wide to *your* strength, don't go for the big shot. The lob is safer and gives more time to recover.

Don't hit every ball at the obvious opening. Occasionally, hit a ball to the spot from which your opponent is coming. If you catch him on the wrong foot because he is going in the opposite direction, he will not be able to touch the ball even though it is only two feet away from him.

Never rush yourself nor allow your opponent to rush you. The player who is trailing will hurry himself too often on the service. If your opponent serves before you are ready, hold up your hand and ask him to play the ball over (you may not ask him to play the ball over if you have returned it). To keep yourself from rushing on your own service, bounce the ball once after you have taken the service position. Serving before you are ready is the fastest way to lose a point.

If you are winning by playing from the baseline, don't start coming to net. If you are winning by coming in on every service, don't start staying back. In other words, never change a winning game just to show what a well-rounded player you are. Conversely, if you are losing, try making adjustments in your strategy, but never switch to a game you do not know how to play. If you are basically a baseliner, don't become a net-rusher after losing a set. Try change of pace: more lobs, softer shots, or a switch from playing your opponent's backhand to playing his forehand.

Vary your game to the conditions. Shorten your strokes on a

23

fast court, play more steadily on a slow court; hit harder when you are playing against the wind and softer when you are playing with it.

Vary your game to the score. If your opponent has 40-0 on his serve, try your big forehand "winner." If you are down 30-40 on your own serve, make sure your first serve goes in. This is a vital point which may make the difference between winning and losing the set. It is therefore not the time to try a difficult shot.

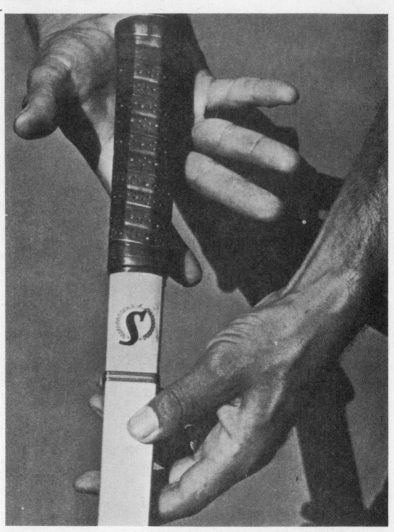

2. FOREHAND GRIP

1. I cradle the throat of the racket in my left hand. The butt of the racket rests on the heel of my hand.

2. I shake hands with the racket, my fingers curved around naturally, the forefinger extending up the racket.

3. The fingers are not bunched together. The forefinger and the thumb wind diagonally across the racket just as in the handshake.

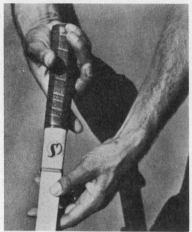

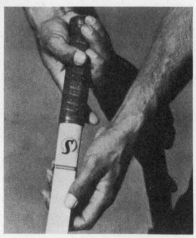

4. Outside view. This shows the natural position of my fingers. Once I have found my grip, I hold the racket tightly.

5. Inside view. I hold the racket head parallel to the ground, which makes for a decided angle between arm and racket.

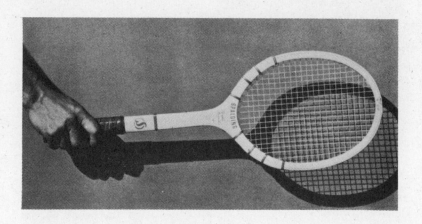

6. If you place your hand flat against the strings and then move it down the handle, gripping it at the end, the correct position of the palm will come naturally.

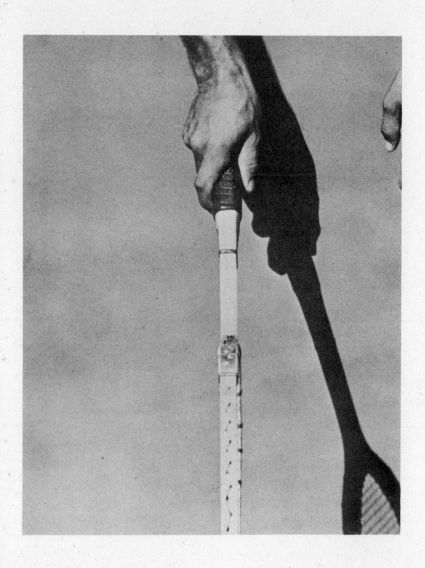

3. FOREHAND DRIVE

Side

1. I see the ball coming to my forehand. I turn sideways and release the fingers of my left hand from the throat of the racket.

2. I am starting my backswing. My weight is on my back foot (I get added power on the hit by shifting weight exactly at the moment of impact from back foot to front foot).

3. This is the end of my backswing. I take a circular backswing with the racket head high, but note that the head will be parallel to the ground (not cocked upward) when I hit. My hips and shoulders have not yet started to pivot.

4. I am leaning forward to meet the ball. I hit it in front of me rather than directly by my side. My wrist is laid back so that racket and arm are at an angle. My hips and shoulders have pivoted so that my body is facing the net. My weight has just been transferred to the front foot.

5. This is the follow-through. My arm and racket are now in one line and are not at an angle. My knees are still bent, since I do not straighten until the very end of the follow-through.

6. With a powerful stroke, the follow-through is often this long. Then it ends over my left shoulder with the racket head quite high.

Front

7. I like to get ready for my forehand whenever possible by turning sideways, even though at the moment of impact my body faces the net.

8. You can see the start of my circular backswing. I use this swing whenever I have ample time to hit the ball.

9. The ball is coming rather slowly, so that I can take as big and free a backswing as I desire. If the ball were coming faster, I would shorten the backswing and the racket head would not be so high.

10. My forward swing has started, and the racket head is now almost parallel to the ground. The wrist is laid back so that arm and racket form an angle. My hips are just about to pivot.

11. At the hit, three things have happened. The weight has been transferred completely to my left foot, and my hips and shoulders have pivoted.

12. This is the follow-through. The knees are still bent, and my racket head is pointing toward the top of my opponent's fence. I often end the stroke here rather than following through over my left shoulder.

4. BACKHAND GRIP

1. This is the backhand grip. It is also essentially the grip used on service, volley and overhead. To obtain it, I cradle the throat of the racket in my left hand. Then my right hand moves counterclockwise (left) a quarter of a turn. The V between thumb and forefinger is no longer on the right of the racket handle, but is slightly to the left.

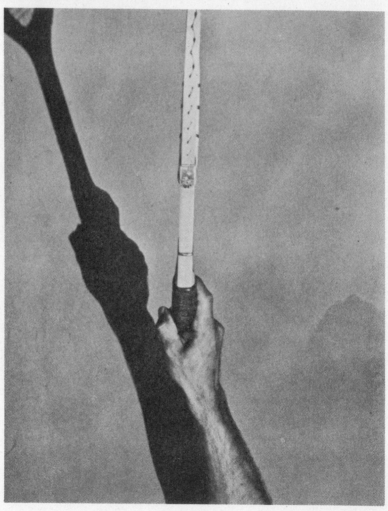

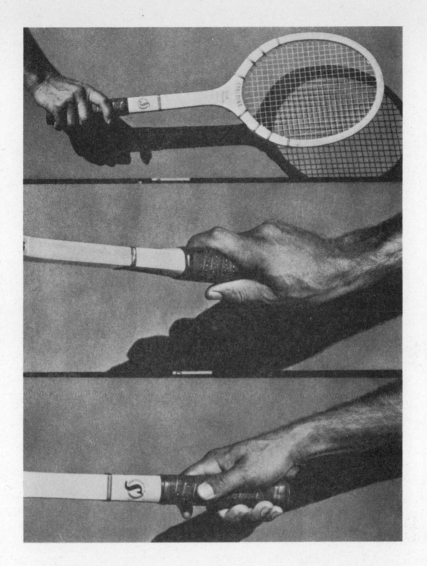

2. The fingers are slightly spread. I try not to bunch them together. I tend to keep my thumb up the racket handle, but many champions prefer to move it one inch further around.

3. Outside view. There is a slight break in the wrist. In other words, the racket and arm are not one straight line.

4. Inside view. The forefinger is clearly separated from the rest of the hand. The thumb slants forward, but is not straight up the racket handle.

5 . BACKHAND DRIVE

Side

1. My ready position is the same for forehand and backhand. The racket throat is cradled in the fingers of my left hand. My knees are slightly flexed, and my feet are well apart. I watch the ball come off my opponent's racket so that I will be ready to turn in either direction.

2. The ball is coming to my backhand. I am just beginning to take my racket back, and my left foot has started its sideways motion.

3. My shoulders are beginning to turn sideways, and I am lifting my right foot off the ground preparatory to moving it forward. I am still cradling the racket with my left hand.

4. My body is now completely sideways to the net. I have taken my right arm all the way back and am ready to swing forward for the hit. My knees are bent, and I am about to transfer my weight to the right foot as I hit.

5. I meet the ball in front of my right foot, not by my side. The racket head is parallel to the ground, and there is a sharp angle between arm and racket. The elbow is practically unbent. My eyes have never left the ball.

Front

1. My side is always to the net when I hit my backhand. I turn as soon as possible. I try to keep my knees bent, particularly on low balls. If the ball is extremely low, the racket head does not point down; instead, I bend even further.

2. I like to take a wide stance on a low ball. My right foot is at least three feet in front of my left one. Note that I do not step sideways, but that I move *toward* the net whenever possible.

3. This is the end of my follow-through. My knees are still bent, my eyes follow the flight of the ball, and I am ready to hop into position for the next shot. The angle between arm and racket has been maintained throughout the stroke.

6. RUNNING FOREHAND DRIVE

1. I can see that I have to run wide for this forehand. My knees are bent and my feet separated. I push off with my left foot, and in so doing, I get a fast start.

2. As I run, I start my backswing. I do not wait until I get to the ball, since I intend to meet it rather than to have the ball meet me.

3. The racket is beginning its backward motion. I am moving toward the ball with long strides. I try to time my strides so that I can plant my left foot when I hit the ball.

4. My eyes never leave the ball. I am now one step away from it. My backswing will be on the short side, since I only take a big backswing when I have plenty of time.

5. I have arrived at the right spot with my backswing completed. I would have preferred to step toward the hit, but when I am running sideways it is impossible.

6. The ball is low, and therefore I have bent my knees quite a bit. My racket head will not point downward just because the ball is low, since that would be a shovel stroke rather than a drive. My wrist is laid all the way back.

7. The stroke is finished, and I am just beginning to straighten up. This time, my follow-through will come almost toward my left shoulder. I will have to move fast to be ready for the next ball, since my entire left court is now open.

7. RUNNING BACKHAND DRIVE

1. Here I see that I must run diagonally forward for a backhand. I push off with my left foot, which is the best way to get a quick start (if I had to run sideways for a backhand, I would push with my right foot).

2. As I run, I begin to take my racket back. I must start my backswing *before* I get to the ball.

3. I am now using my left hand to take the racket back. I am one step from the ball and have judged my stride so that I will be on my right foot when I hit.

4. My left hand is still acting as a guide as my racket goes
back. The racket head is high on the backswing, but it will be
parallel to the ground on the hit.

5. My right foot has stepped toward the net as much as
possible. I will be hitting the ball not just with arm and racket,
but with my entire weight. I will hit the ball in front of me with
the face of my racket parallel to the net.

6. The racket head never drops. The arm and the racket form an angle at all times. The elbow is almost completely straight from the moment I hit the ball until I complete the follow-through.

7. This is the end of the follow-through. The racket head points to the top of my opponent's fence. During the entire sequence, my eyes have never left the ball. Watching the ball is synonymous with good concentration.

8. HIGH BACKHAND

1. In this high backhand sequence, follow my head motion and you will see that my eyes never leave the ball. My backswing will be higher, but the motion is identical to the low backhand action.

2. In order to pivot properly, I will move one step back so that I can then move into the ball. I never want to hit a ball when moving backwards.

3. I took one giant step back, and I will now be able to move into the ball with my right foot. My object is to keep my side to the net when I hit my backhand.

4. My racket head is going to come back over my shoulder, since I will be hitting the ball at shoulder height. I will swing *up* at the ball rather than down at it.

5. My left hand is guiding the racket all the way back. My weight is still on my left foot, but my right foot is beginning to move forward.

6. My backswing is finished, and I am about to hit *up* on the ball. If I hit downward while standing behind the baseline, my shot would inevitably be too short.

7. The hit is finished, and my weight is on my front foot. As always on the backhand drive, the racket head points to the top of my opponent's fence.

9. SERVICE AND OVERHEAD GRIP

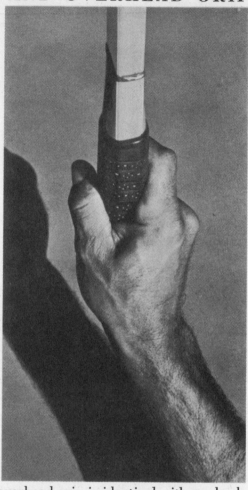

1. My service and overhead grip is identical with my backhand grip except that my thumb is more around the racket handle. The forefinger is separated from the other fingers, and the racket forms an angle with the arm.

2. Almost every champion, man or woman, has used this grip for service and overhead. Don't use the forehand grip, since it will prevent you from obtaining real power or good spin control.

10. SERVE

1. I start my service with a straight back. I do not sway forward in a rocking motion as I start my toss.

45

2. My toss started at waist height and went directly up. At no time did my left hand ever drop below waist level.

3. My knees bend forward, rather than sideways or in two different directions. ⟩

47

4. The backbend should not be overdone. Some players arch far too much, thereby overtaxing the muscles.

5. I never "cheat" on my grip by moving toward the fore-hand side. This would take away my power.

6. My wrist breaks back sharply, and I am up on both toes to get an extra "kick" action.

7. From this frame and the next one, you can see how my racket moves across the ball to my right to give it American twist.

8. I hit with my right foot in the air, since I swing it over the line when I follow my serve to net.

9. My follow-through is across my left leg, and I have started to move toward the net.

Side

1. I start the service with the toe of my left foot pointing toward the net near the center service line. My body is sideways to the net, and my legs are almost two feet apart. I have already started my motion, since my racket arm has begun to move away from my left hand.

2. Left and right hands move in rhythm. The left arm will move slowly straight up, while the right arm, traveling slightly faster, will make a long, sweeping circle. The ball does not leave the fingers of my left hand until my arm is fully extended.

3. The ball has left my fingertips (I hold it over, rather than in, the palm of my hand). I place the ball in a line with my right shoulder, but slightly in front of it. The height of my toss will be that point where my right arm and racket, fully extended, can hit it. I never toss the ball so high that I have to wait for it to drop.

4. My knees are bent slightly forward, but my weight has not yet come through. I arch my back slightly. When I hit, my knees and my back will be absolutely straight. In other words, I am coming up on the ball with all my weight.

5. My right foot begins to move forward, since I will hit with both feet almost together. My racket arm has finished its big, sweeping circle, and I am going to drop the racket head behind my back. My tossing arm is descending naturally.

6. The racket head is so far back that it almost scratches my back. At this stage my knees are almost straight, since all of me is moving up toward the ball. My elbow is bent back as far as it can go.

7. The racket head is now moving high into the air. My elbow will straighten and my wrist will snap forward as I meet the ball. My right shoulder will pivot forward. This means that the ball will be hit with racket, wrist, arm and shoulder, as well as with my knees and body.

8. If you compare the previous frame with this frame, you will see how my wrist has snapped forward. You can see that my body was fully extended. As I hit the ball, my racket face rolled around and to my right, which gave it a small amount of American twist spin. Sometimes I slice the ball by moving my racket face toward my left. I prefer either of these two spins to an absolutely flat ball, since they give me more control (completely flat balls just don't go in the court).

9. My racket will swing around my left leg as the follow-through is completed. My right foot stays behind the baseline, since I did not intend to come into net behind this service. Note that my hips came forward as well as my shoulders.

11. OVERHEAD

1. A beginner must learn to hit overheads immediately, since the smash is a basic stroke. However, he should not try too big an action until he learns to time the ball properly. From the very beginning, though, he must use the right grip.

2. As in every tennis stroke, the feet must always be separated. My knees are flexed and my side is toward the net as I await the approach of the ball. I can skip forward or backward as necessary when I see the ball begin to drop.

3. Beginners should take a short backswing until timing becomes secure. I turn my wrist around so that I can hit the ball quite flat. It is desirable to use as little spin as possible, since overheads are taken from well inside the baseline and therefore one can afford to hit straight down.

4. Here I demonstrate the small punch. Until you can get every overhead in the court and place it well, you should not use a bigger stroke. I never flailed away with all my power until I first had achieved consistency and placement.

5. I am getting ready for a full-swing overhead. My racket position is the same as it is for service. I have moved to approximately the right spot, and my legs are very far apart. Most beginners are afraid to stretch wide with bent legs, but if they practice regularly on stretching low and wide, they will improve their balance, reach and position play.

6. I am making last-minute adjustments with my feet as I judge the trajectory of the ball. Although the overhead action is very much like the service, in the former case one is playing against a moving target which may be spinning.

64

7. My overhead wind-up is small when compared to my
service. There is no big round-house circular motion. The
racket is lifted straight up. My left arm goes up, since I always
point to the ball before I hit. This gives me balance and better judgment.

8. Here I am, knees flexed, back bent, left arm pointing toward the ball for balance, and right arm going back for the
vital part of the wind-up. This frame by itself could be taken
for part of a service sequence, as could the succeeding ones.

9. My left arm has come down, and my right arm is pic-
tured at the terminal point of the backswing. The racket is
practically scratching my back, which is slightly arched. My
right leg is moving forward, although my weight has not yet
been transferred.

10. I turn my wrist as I hit. I use no spin, since I am standing inside the service line and can hit flat and down while still clearing the net with safety. This was not a difficult lob, since I did not have to jump for it. Tough lobs are those that land close to the baseline, forcing the player to run back and leap or take the ball on the bounce.

11. The follow-through is across my left leg, just as in the service. From this position my chances are good for hitting an outright winner, but my opponent may have anticipated me, and I must be ready for his return. Never act as though the point is over until the ball is actually out of play.

12. FOREHAND VOLLEY

1. The ready position at net is exactly the same as the ready position in the backcourt. The throat of the racket is cradled in the left hand, the racket head points upward, the knees are flexed, and I bend forward without losing good balance.

2. The volley action is much shorter than the groundstroke. There should be almost no backswing and very little follow-through. The entire shot can be as small as a one-foot punch. If time permits, I try to have my left foot stepping forward, although in a fast exchange at net this is sometimes impossible.

3. Here I have taken a rather big backswing. The ball is high, and I have plenty of time. However, my racket *never* moved behind my body, even at the furthest point of the backswing. My wrist is just starting to move forward, and I will be able to hit the ball well in front of me.

4. I try to step toward the net rather than sideways. I am hitting the ball at least one foot in front of me. The stroke ends almost immediately, with my racket moving no more than another foot or two. Even with this short jab, we can get great power.

1. I like to emphasize the ready stance, which is the basic position in tennis. You cannot meet the ball well, nor can you pivot properly, if your knees and back are straight and your feet are together. Also, the racket should never dangle helplessly in front of you, and the head should always be up.

2. This is going to be a low backhand volley. I get down to the ball by bending my knees, since I don't like to drop my racket head. This is the entire backswing. The racket never gets behind me at all.

3. I am still crouched, but my right foot moves forward as I hit the ball one foot in front of me. The ball is almost at net level, so I cannot hit down or even swing flat. I therefore tilt the racket face so that the ball will travel up and over the net.

4. Here you can see by the bevel of my racket face what must be done on all low volleys. This is the natural short follow-through of a slice volley.

5. This is my complete backswing on a slightly higher backhand volley. I support the racket with the fingers of my left hand, and I plan to hit the ball well in front of me.

6. I have time to step forward with my right foot. It is a waist-high volley, and I do not hit down on the ball since it would not clear the net if I did. Instead, I open the racket face slightly to give the ball a little underspin.

14. FOREHAND HALF-VOLLEY

1. Anyone who comes to net, either in singles or doubles, will occasionally have to half-volley. This stroke is a shortened version of the forehand in which the ball is hit immediately after it bounces. I must crouch down, since I take the ball right off the ground. I use the forehand grip, but my backswing starts practically at my side.

2. The ball is taken so low that the racket head must drop slightly. I hit it well in front of me, keeping my eye on it and guiding the racket with my wrist. The half-volley is never a hard stroke. Note that my right knee is less than a foot from the ground.

3. I have pivoted, but I am still down as low as in the previous frame. I don't straighten until after the follow-through, which is extremely short. I end the stroke with the racket head beveled up, since I have to lift a low ball over the net.

4. One half-volleys not through choice, but through neces-
sity. Hence, the half-volley often is executed from awkward
positions. Here I am too close to the ball, which is coming
straight at me.

5. Because I am so close, I cannot bend my knees as much
as I would like. I am forced to bend from the waist in order
to get down to the ball, coming directly at me.

6. I end the stroke with the smallest possible follow-
through, guiding it with a laid-back wrist. I must open the face
of the racket to get the ball over the net.

15. BACKHAND HALF-VOLLEY

1. I use the backhand grip, taking my racket back with my left hand.

2. I get down to the ball as far as I can, taking a very short backswing.

3. My left knee is less than a foot from the ground. My
right foot steps toward the net.

4. The ball is hit well in front of me. The racket and arm form a sharp angle.

5. The racket face opens up in order to lift the ball above net height. I remain crouched through the short follow-through.

16. SERVING AND RECEIVING POSITIONS

SINGLES

Serve to the backhand!

When I am serving in the forehand court in singles, I stand in Position A (right next to the center service line). I aim for Section E of the court, which means deep to my opponent's backhand. All second serves should be aimed for Section E. Only rarely should you try to hit to Section F—e.g., when your opponent no longer expects it.

When I serve in the backhand court, I stand at Position B, which is not quite as close to the center service line. This allows me the proper angle to hit to Section G. I aim for Section G almost always, since this is my opponent's backhand. Only on rare occasions do I try for Section H.

Try for *depth* on the service. You lose all advantage if your delivery is short.

When serving to a left-hander, the positions are reversed. I stand slightly away from the center service line in the forehand court, and right by the center service line in the backhand court.

When I receive in the forehand court, I stand in Position C. When I receive in the backhand court, I stand in Position D.

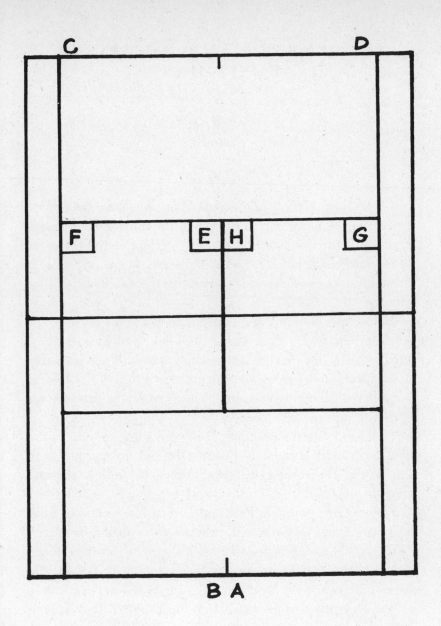

17. SERVING AND RECEIVING POSITIONS

DOUBLES

In doubles, I serve from a position approximately three feet from the alley line (Position A for the forehand court, Position B for the backhand court). Again, one tries to serve to the backhand, but it is not as hard and fast a rule as it is in singles. Occasional wide serves to the forehand can be effective.

My partner should stand in Position E when I serve in the forehand court. He must cover his alley, and he should be fairly close to the net, but not hanging over it. When he learns to leap well on the volley, he can stand in Position G. Here he is better situated for covering the entire left court and for handling lobs over his head.

The same relative positions are taken when serving in the backhand court. I stand in Position B, and my partner is in Position F. He moves to H when he feels his volley is strong enough.

The receiver stands in Position C when I serve in the forehand court and in Position D when I serve in the backhand court. As the receiver becomes more sure of his return, he moves to Position X for the forehand and Position Y for the backhand (*inside* the baseline). The receiver's partner stands at net just as my partner does. He is in Position I when I serve in the forehand court (until he is capable of handling himself in Position K), and he stands in Position J when I serve in the backhand court (until he can handle Position L).

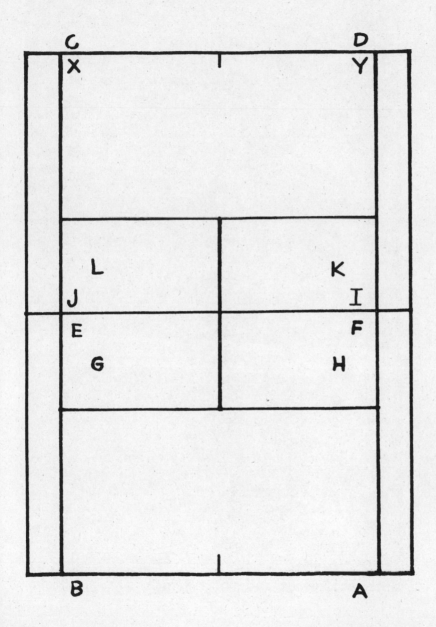

18. COMING TO NET

COMING IN ON SERVICE

The beginner must work on coming in on his serve in doubles. He should never come in on his serve in singles until he is an accomplished volleyer. In doubles, he has less court to cover and it is not as difficult.

The serve should have plenty of spin so that the beginner has time to get himself into the service court area for his first volley. He should never hit on the dead run. He runs in after serving, stops, and then takes one step forward as he volleys (he steps forward with his left foot on the forehand volley, and with his right foot on the backhand volley).

After he hits his first volley, which he should generally aim deep down the center, he should take two more steps forward so that he will have the advantage of being closer in.

Sometimes, when the beginner comes in on his serve, the ball bounces at his feet. He should try, if at all possible, to get in a little faster so that he can volley it; if he cannot, then he should step back a few feet and hit the ball as a ground stroke. He should avoid the half-volley as much as possible, since it is a defensive stroke.

A player must come to net when his opponent hits him a short ball. If the ball bounces *high and short*, the player may be able to end the point then and there. He should take his time, using a full stroke, stepping toward the net as he hits and placing the ball with accuracy. However, if the ball is low, the player will have to lift it over the net by opening the face of his racket on his backhand and hitting with overspin on his forehand. This means he cannot hit it very hard. He must hit the ball with depth (as close to his opponent's baseline as possible).

If the low, short ball comes to the forehand side, the player hits a forehand down the line, as close as possible to the baseline-alley area of the court. The opponent is then forced to hit a backhand passing shot. The player stands to the right of the center service line, which is the best position from which to cut off backhand passing shots.

Player A runs in for a short low forehand 1. He tries to hit for Box X. After he hits, he moves to Position A-1 in order to cover all possible backhand passing shots.

If the low, short ball bounces to his backhand but is not too far from the center 2, Player A again aims for Box X, then moves to Position A-1.

If the ball bounces wide to the backhand 3, Player A must hit his backhand down the line to the area marked by Y. After the hit, he moves to Position B in order to cover all forehand passing shots.

You should *never* hit to Box Y when the ball bounces low and short to the forehand 1, since you are leaving your entire backhand court open. Similarly, don't hit from 3 to Box X, since you are exposing your entire forehand side.

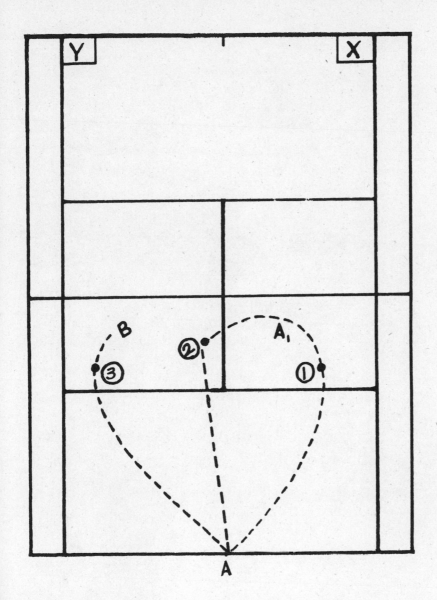

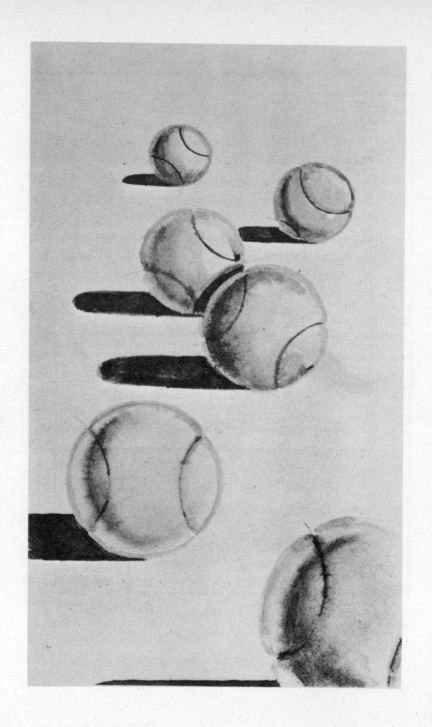

19. DROPSHOT AND LOB

It is possible to play good tennis without having a dropshot, but the lob is basic to intelligent play. It is used both defensively and offensively, and it is an important weapon.

The lob is a controlled ground stroke in which the face of the racket opens. The trajectory is high, the idea being to lift the ball over the opponent's head. One aims close to the opponent's baseline, and the highest spot in the trajectory is roughly over the net (mid-way in the flight of the ball).

The lob should be hit with disguise if it is to be an offensive shot. The opponent, who is at net, can then be caught flatfooted because he is expecting an attempted passing shot.

The defensive lob is used when you are pulled far out of court or a ball comes so deep and hard to you that you cannot make an accurate lower return. Don't be ashamed to throw up a sky-ball (a ball that goes 30 feet into the air) if it will get you back into position and back into the play. The greatest players in the world do it when they are in serious trouble.

The dropshot is hit with a volley action. The idea is to make the ball barely drop over the net and then die. The face of the racket must be open, as though you were hitting a low volley with backspin.

Never hit a dropshot when you are behind the baseline. If you develop a good dropshot, use it when you are inside the service line and your opponent is on or behind the baseline.

Don't dropshot too often. The value of this stroke is the element of surprise.

If your opponent returns the dropshot, your parry is the lob. He has been running forward, and now he has to reverse himself to run back.

20. BASELINE RALLIES

When you are learning to play, the most important factor is steadiness. The ball must go into the court. Stroke it (don't push it or shove it), but get it over the net. Don't try to hit it hard. Don't try tricky shots.

When I was learning to play, I tried at first to get the ball over the net at least 10 times without missing. Once I achieved this, it was very simple to hit the ball in the court 100 times.

When you are consistent, and when every ball goes in the court area, then try for depth. Hit the ball close to the baseline. Don't hit it inside the service line. The ball should go high over the net, clearing it by 3 to 5 feet. If your ball barely skims the net, it will fall short of the baseline.

Once you have achieved consistency and depth, try for placement. First, work on your crosscourts. Hit every forehand to your opponent's forehand. Remember, though, that the ball must go in and the ball must be deep. Then practice hitting your backhand to your opponent's backhand. Clear the net by a large margin and make sure your ball goes deep. Hit the ball well in front of you when aiming crosscourt. You cannot hit good crosscourts if you meet the ball by your side.

Although the crosscourt is the basic groundstroke shot, you must also be able to hit the ball down the line. On the forehand, keep your side to the net, stepping in with your left foot as you hit. The moment of impact is one fraction of a second later than on the crosscourt, more to the side, and not as much in front of you. The same procedure applies to the backhand down the line.

Never try to hit the ball hard. When your crosscourts and down-the-line shots are consistent and accurate, concentrate on proper weight transference, which will give you natural pace. On the forehand I step toward the net with my left foot just before the hit, using a hip-shoulder pivot to put all my weight behind the ball. On the backhand I step in with my right foot, transferring my weight at the hit to my right shoulder and right foot.

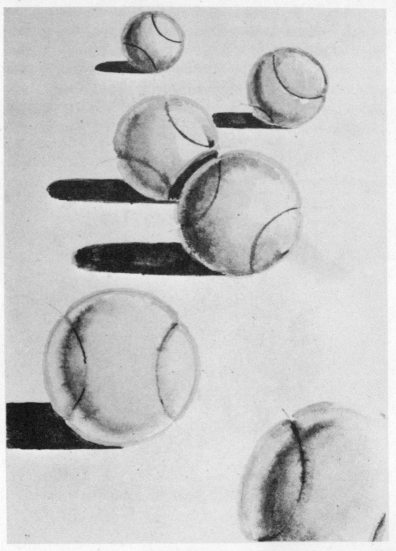

21. PRACTICING

The backboard is a wonderful means of developing consistency and of practicing a given ground stroke. When you use it, work on one stroke at a time. I hit only forehands for 10 minutes, hopping back or forward as necessary. The backboard doesn't miss, and in 10 minutes you will have a real workout. Then work on your backhand; try for consistency and remember to step in toward the board on each stroke. Don't hit too low against the backboard. Aim for an area well above the net line.

Serving an occasional box of balls on the court works miracles. Take the empty box or a folded towel and make it your target. Place it in the backhand corner of a service court.

Before you play sets, try to groove your ground strokes from the backcourt and your volley from the net. Don't neglect the volley, since it is as necessary to your game as forehand or backhand.

Ask your opponent to hit you at least six overheads before you start a match. Do the same for him, as it will help you learn a controlled lob.

22. FOOTWORK

The knees must always be flexed and the feet far apart. Never stand stiff-legged. When running to the side, push off on the back foot (when running to the right, push off on the left foot; when running to the left, push off on the right foot). Don't stand flatfooted. Bounce lightly on your toes so that you can be ready to push off quickly in any direction.

Skip sideways to the ball when you have ample time. This automatically ends you on the proper foot after each move.

If you have to pivot backward in order to get into position, don't forget to take one step toward the net as you meet the ball.

23. SUMMARY

1. Watch the ball come off your opponent's racket.

2. Keep your knees flexed and your legs a good eighteen inches apart.

3. Start your backswing early so that you can meet the ball rather than having the ball meet you.

4. Bend your knees. Try to step in (toward the net) as you hit. Step in with your left foot on the forehand and with your right foot on the backhand.

5. Never let your weight move back on any tennis stroke. If your weight is not transferred forward, the ball is moving you rather than you moving the ball.

6. Stay down to the ball with knees flexed throughout the hit. Don't straighten until the end of the follow-through.

7. When the follow-through is completed, hop or slide into position immediately so you can be ready for the next shot.

8. Use change of pace. Don't hit each ball with the same amount of speed or spin. This will give your harder balls the element of surprise.

9. Vary your service 20% to the forehand, 80% to the backhand of the time, even if the forehand is your opponent's weakness.

10. When you play a better player, *don't try to hit harder*. Play your own game, but try to be faster on your feet.

11. Your first serve should go in at least 70% of the time.

12. Never change a winning game.

13. On windy days, hit harder when the wind is against you. Use spin to keep the ball in court when the wind is behind you.

14. Hit deep balls back deep rather than hard. Your chance for placements will come when your opponent hits short.

15. The overhead should be placed, not slugged.

16. Watch your position on the court. Play several feet behind the baseline if your opponent is hitting deep; stand inside the baseline by several feet if your opponent is servng short.

17. Don't rush yourself on the serve.

18. When your opponent is at net, hit low; when he is in the back court, clear the net by at least 3 to 5 feet.

19. Disguise your shots.

20. Don't be too proud to retrieve.

APPENDIX

EQUIPMENT

As a beginning tennis player, you should purchase the proper equipment and be prepared to take care of it conscientiously; if you follow these rules, your initial expense will be a wise investment in terms of durability and satisfaction. Not only is tennis one of the least expensive sports in which you can participate (even if you buy the best equipment!), but also one of the most rewarding in the amount of exercise and challenge it offers. Your knowledge of equipment probably will be limited at the outset, so you will find an expert in a tennis shop or the tennis department of any well-stocked sporting goods store of invaluable assistance with advice on the latest gear and how to make the selections that will be right for you.

There is one cardinal rule to follow in buying equipment— don't skimp! You will discover that buying the cheapest racket, tennis balls and shoes does not pay off in the long run; they will have to be replaced much too soon.

THE RACKET

The major item, of course, is the racket, and this is where some skilled advice is most essential, since these are so many excellent rackets from which to choose. A wise procedure is inspection of all makes, weights and grip sizes, as there is no strict formula to follow in selecting a racket—merely your own individual preference, aided by some informed guidance from the expert.

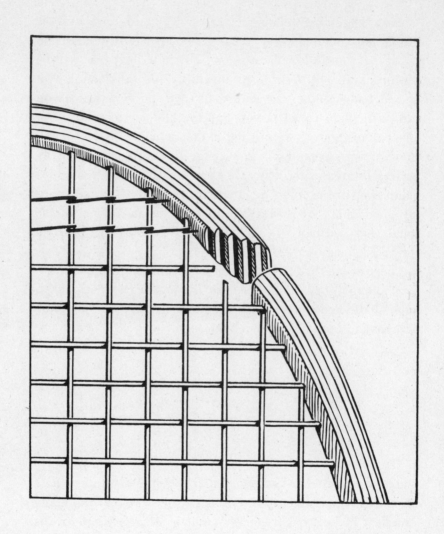

The Frame

Frames are almost always made of wood, ash being one of the favorites. Standard frame prices and quality vary with the type and grade of wood and the number of laminations (ply), which can range from 1 to 11. A new trend is toward the fiberglass frame, which will not warp in humidity, and therefore has a major advantage over the wooden one; this frame is still in the development stage.

Stringing

Your strings may be made of silk, nylon, hog gut or lamb gut; silk and nylon are economical for the beginner because of their relative resistance to climatic conditions, but champion players favor gut because of the extra bite it gives their shots. There is a new development in strings, also: perfected nylon, which will have the same advantage as the fiberglass frame— it will not deteriorate in damp weather. If you choose gut stringing, let the expert be the judge of the correct gauge of the gut and the tension to which it is strung; these two factors are rather complex for the beginner to grasp by himself.

Don't forget an important rule for prolonging the life of your stringing—try to play on dry courts. The more water your strings pick up from the tennis ball, the shorter their life.

Weight

The weight of your racket is a highly individual matter. You may find yourself confused at first trying to distinguish among the $\frac{1}{4}$-ounce variations in weight, so it may help to think simply in terms of light, medium and heavy. Racket weights vary from about $11\frac{1}{2}$ ounces for the young beginner to about $14\frac{1}{2}$ ounces for an experienced player who can handle that weight; approximate averages are $13\frac{1}{4}$-$14\frac{1}{2}$ ounces for men, $\frac{1}{4}$ ounce less for women, and 12-13 ounces for younger players. Try holding and swinging as many rackets as you can find in the tennis shop until you (and the expert!) decide on the right weight for you. Your first racket may be on the light side, but try to pick the heaviest one that feels comfortable to you (it will improve your game).

Balance

This factor is a matter on which your tennis pro can be extremely helpful. Since the racket is 27 inches long, the true balance point would be $13\frac{1}{2}$ inches from the bottom of the handle; the best performing rackets are those which balance from 13 to $13\frac{3}{4}$ inches from the bottom.

Grip Size

Grip sizes vary by $\frac{1}{8}$ inch and range from about $4\frac{3}{8}$ to 5 inches. The same rules that are recommended for testing racket weights apply to grips. Try many sizes to see which feels natural in your hand. Some experts feel that an ideal handle is one around which your thumb can cover the nail of your third finger; this is another individual matter.

Cover and Press

If you want to take the best possible care of your racket, these two items are indispensable. They should be in place on your racket whenever you are not actually playing tennis. Many covers are made with a pocket for tennis balls, eliminating some extra carrying. The press is exactly what its name implies, a wooden or metal frame that slides over the racket head and then is secured tightly in place. The type with a centered lever arrangement is preferable to that with four corner screws, as it is not always possible to obtain equal tension on the frame with the latter. A press is essential if you intend to avoid letting your racket warp.

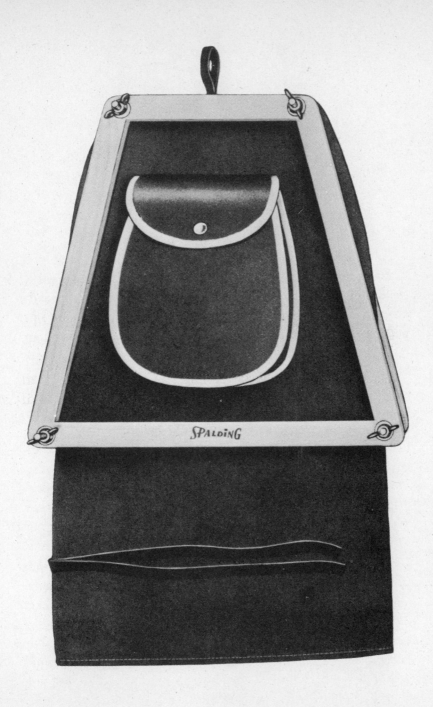

Tennis Balls

There are as many brands of tennis balls as there are rackets, but each year the U. S. Lawn Tennis Association approves about a dozen of them, so you can't go far wrong. An important new development in tennis balls is the new Swedish make, which are not vacuum-packed; they maintain their balance for an amazingly long time, they have a wonderful bounce, and they are relatively inexpensive. No matter which brand you play with, don't try to save money by using the same balls forever; your game won't be helped by tennis balls that have lost their bounce and speed. When the fuzzy outer covering begins to disappear, the tennis ball will start losing its liveliness.

Tennis requires as much practice as you can give it; obviously, practicing with a partner is ideal, but unfortunately, a partner can't always be found. Many tennis clubs, municipal courts and playgrounds have backboards to practice on. If a backboard isn't available, there are some new devices which are very helpful, among them an automatic ball return and a special net which returns your balls. The net device even makes it possible to practice your serve. Neither device requires a court, so they are especially useful in a limited space.

Two words serve as common denominators for the right tennis clothes—"white" and "neat." Although colors are worn sometimes in very informal play, court tradition and etiquette demand white for tournament and match play; following suit, many hotels, resorts and tennis clubs insist on *white only* on their courts. There are some practical reasons behind this tradition: white reflects, rather than absorbs, heat, thus helping the player to stay cool; also, the uniform wearing of white is not distracting to other players, as bright colors might be. Neatness is important in this active sport—shirts hanging sloppily out of shorts are tabu!

Shoes and Socks

Shoes are the most important part of your tennis clothes—don't buy the cheapest pair you can find. The ideal pair is durable and light with smoothly molded (no treads) soles for skidproof traction. Don't substitute basketball or other sports shoes—you can easily find many brands made solely for playing *tennis!* Don't forget to put on a pair of tennis socks before trying on a new pair of shoes, as the proper pair of wool socks will take up some room (some players wear two pairs for playing on hard courts). Since your socks will be white, you will avoid infection from dye if you should develop blisters.

Men's Clothes

Although in cool climates long, flannel trousers are still worn often, the usual attire for men, both in tournament and informal play, now consists of T-shirt (always tucked in!) and tailored shorts (almost Bermuda length).

Women's Clothes

Although many women wear the shirt-and-shorts combination for informal games, almost all tournament players wear a tennis dress, a one-piece outfit about the same length as shorts. Most of these dresses are so attractive that some women have been known to take up the game just to wear one!

Sweat Bands

Tennis is a strenuous game, and for those who perspire profusely, sweat bands can be very helpful. These are small, cotton-knit elasticized strips worn around one or both wrists; they serve to keep moisture off the player's hands (and therefore off his racket).

Miscellaneous

Some players may want to buy a tennis cap with visor to keep the sun out of their eyes, if they don't wear sunglasses. Many wear neither, as they find them more of a hindrance than a help. Anything loose (such as jewelry) can be very distracting.

DIAGRAM AND DIMENSIONS OF TENNIS COURT

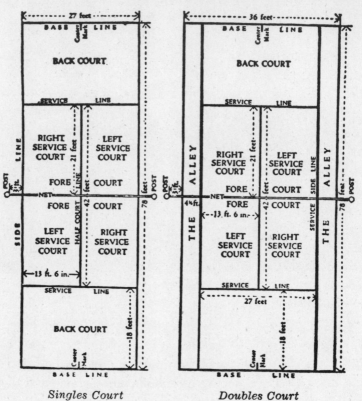

Singles Court   Doubles Court

RULES OF LAWN TENNIS

THE SINGLES GAME

RULE 1

Dimensions and Equipment

The court shall be a rectangle, 78 feet long and 27 feet wide. It shall be divided across the middle by a net, suspended from a cord or metal cable of a maximum diameter of ⅓ inch, the ends of which shall be attached to, or pass over, the tops of two posts, 3 feet 6 inches high, the center of which shall be 3 feet outside the court on each side. The height of the net shall be 3 feet at the center, where it shall be held down taut by a strap not more than 2 inches wide. There shall be a band covering the cord or metal cable and the top of the net not less than 2 inches nor more than 2½ inches in depth on each side. The lines bounding the ends and sides of the court shall, respectively, be called the baselines and sidelines. On each side of the net, at a distance of 21 feet from it and parallel with it, shall be drawn the service lines. The space on each side of the net between the service line and the sidelines shall be divided into two equal parts called the service courts by the center service line, which must be 2 inches in width, drawn halfway between, and parallel with, the sidelines. Each baseline shall be bisected by an imaginary continuation of the center service line to a line 4 inches in length and 2 inches in width called the center mark drawn inside the court, at right angles to and in contact with such baselines. All other lines shall not be less than 1 inch nor more than 2 inches in width, except the baseline, which may be 4 inches in width, and all measurements shall be made to the outside of the lines.

Rule 2

Permanent Fixtures

The permanent fixtures of the court shall include not only the net, posts, cord or metal cable, strap and band, but also, where there are any such, the back and side stops, the stands, fixed or movable seats and chairs around the court, and their occupants, all other fixtures around and above the court, and the umpire, foot-fault judge and linesmen when in their respective places.

Rule 3

Ball—Size, Weight and Bound

The ball shall have a uniform outer surface. If there are any seams, they shall be stitchless. The ball shall be more than $2\frac{1}{2}$ inches and less than $2\frac{5}{8}$ inches in diameter, and more than 2 ounces and less than 2 1/16 ounces in weight. The ball shall have a bound of more than 53 inches when dropped 100 inches upon a concrete base, and a deformation of more than .265 of an inch and less than .290 of an inch when subjected to a pressure of 18 pounds applied to each end of any diameter.

Rule 4

Server and Receiver

The players shall stand on opposite sides of the net; the player who first delivers the ball shall be called the server, and the other the receiver.

Rule 5

Choice of Sides and Service

The choice of sides and the right to be server or receiver in the first game shall be decided by toss. The player winning the toss may choose or require his opponent to choose:

(a) The right to be server or receiver, in which case the other player shall choose the side; or

(b) The side, in which case the other player shall choose the right to be server or receiver.

Rule 6

Delivery of Service

The service shall be delivered in the following manner. Immediately before commencing to serve, the server shall stand with both feet at rest behind (i.e., further from the net than) the baseline, and within the imaginary continuations of the center mark and sideline. The server shall then project the ball by hand into the air in any direction and before it hits the ground strike it with his racket, and the delivery shall be deemed to have been completed at the moment of the impact of the racket and the ball. A player with the use of only one arm may utilize his racket for the projection.

Rule 7

Foot Fault

The server shall throughout the delivery of the service:

(a) Not change his position by walking or running.

(b) Not touch, with either foot, any area other than that behind the baseline within the imaginary extension of the center mark and sideline.

RULE 8

From Alternate Courts

(a) In delivering the service, the server shall stand alternately behind the right and left courts, beginning from the right in every game. If service from a wrong half of the court occurs and is undetected, all play resulting from such wrong service or services shall stand, but the inaccuracy of the station shall be corrected immediately if it is discovered.
(b) The ball served shall pass over the net and hit the ground within the service court which is diagonally opposite, or upon any line bounding such court, before the receiver returns it.

RULE 9

Faults

The service is a fault:
(a) If the server commit any breach of Rules 6, 7 or 8;
(b) If he miss the ball in attempting to strike it;
(c) If the ball served touch a permanent fixture (other than the net, strap or band) before it hits the ground.

RULE 10

Service After a Fault

After a fault (if it be the first fault), the server shall serve again from behind the same half of the court from which he served that fault, unless the service was from the wrong half, when, in accordance with Rule 8, the server shall be entitled to one service only from behind the other half. A fault may not be claimed after the next service has been delivered.

Rule 11

Receiver Must Be Ready

The server shall not serve until the receiver is ready. If the latter attempt to return the service, he shall be deemed ready. If, however, the receiver signify that he is not ready, he may not claim a fault because the ball does not hit the ground within the limits fixed for the service.

Rule 12

A Let

In all cases where a let has to be called under the rules, or to provide for an interruption to play, it shall have the following interpretation:

(a) When called solely in respect of a service, that one service only shall be replayed.

(b) When called under any other circumstance, the point shall be replayed.

Rule 13

The service is a let:

(a) If the ball served touch the net, strap or band, and is otherwise good, or, after touching the net, strap or band, touch the receiver or anything which he wears or carries before hitting the ground.

(b) If a service or fault be delivered when the receiver is not ready (see Rule 11). In case of a let, that particular service shall not count, and the server shall serve again, but a service let does not annul a previous fault.

RULE 14

When Receiver Becomes Server

At the end of the first game, the receiver shall become the server, and the server, receiver; and so on alternately in all the subsequent games of a match. If a player serve out of turn, the player who ought to have served shall serve as soon as the mistake is discovered, but all points scored before such discovery shall be reckoned. If a game shall have been completed before such discovery, the order of service remains as altered. A fault served before such discovery shall not be reckoned.

RULE 15

Ball in Play Until Point Decided

A ball is in play from the moment at which it is delivered in service. Unless a fault or a let be called, it remains in play until the point is decided.

RULE 16

Server Wins Point

The server wins the point:

(a) If the ball served, not being a let under Rule 13, touch the receiver or anything he wears or carries, before it hits the ground.

(b) If the receiver otherwise lose the point as provided by Rule 18.

RULE 17

Receiver Wins Point

The receiver wins the point:

(a) If the server serve two consecutive faults;

(b) If the server otherwise lose the point as provided by Rule 18.

114

RULE 18

Player Loses Point

A player loses the point if:

(a) He fail, before the ball in play has hit the ground twice consecutively, to return it directly over the net [except as provided in Rule 22 (a) or (c)]; or

(b) He return the ball in play so that it hits the ground, a permanent fixture, or other object, outside any of the lines which bound his opponent's court [except as provided in Rule 22 (a) or (c)]; or

(c) He volley the ball and fail to make a good return even when standing outside the court; or

(d) He touch or strike the ball in play with his racket more than once in making a stroke; or

(e) He or his racket (in his hand or otherwise) or anything which he wears or carries touch the net, posts, cord or metal cable, strap or band, or the ground within his opponent's court at any time while the ball is in play; or

(f) He volley the ball before it has passed the net; or

(g) The ball in play touch him or anything that he wears or carries, except his racket in his hand or hands; or

(h) He throw his racket at and hit the ball.

RULE 19

Player Hinders Opponent

If a player commits any act either deliberate or involuntary which, in the opinion of the umpire, hinders his opponent in making a stroke, the umpire shall in the first case award the point to the opponent, and in the second case order the point to be replayed.

RULE 20

Ball Falling on Line—Good

A ball falling on a line is regarded as falling in the court bounded by that line.

RULE 21

Ball Touching Permanent Fixture

If the ball in play touch a permanent fixture (other than the net, posts, cord or metal cable, strap or band) after it has hit the ground, the player who struck it wins the point; if before it hits the ground, his opponent wins the point.

RULE 22

Good Return

It is a good return:

(a) If the ball touch the net, posts, cord or metal cable, strap or band, provided that it passes over any of them and hits the ground within the court; or

(b) If the ball, served or returned, hit the ground within the proper court and rebound or be blown back over the net, and the player whose turn it is to strike reach over the net and play the ball, provided that neither he nor any part of his clothes or racket touch the net, posts, cord or metal cable, strap or band or the ground within his opponent's court, and that the stroke be otherwise good; or

(c) If the ball be returned outside the post, either above or below the level of the top of the net, even though it touch the post, provided that it hit the ground within the proper court; or

(d) If a player's racket pass over the net after he has returned the ball, provided the ball pass the net before being played and be properly returned; or

(e) If a player succeed in returning the ball, served or in play, which strikes a ball lying in the court.

Rule 23

Interference

In case a player is hindered in making a stroke by anything not within his control except a permanent fixture of the court, or except as provided for in Rule 19, the point shall be replayed.

Rule 24

The Game

If a player wins his first point, the score is called 15 for that player; on winning his second point, the score is called 30 for that player; on winning his third point, the score is called 40 for that player; and the fourth point won by a player is scored *game* for that player except as below:

If both players have won three points, the score is called *deuce,* and the next point won by a player is called *advantage* for that player. If the same player wins the next point, he wins the game; if the other player wins the next point, the score is again called *deuce;* and so on until a player wins the two points immediately following the score at deuce, when the game is scored for that player.

RULE 25

The Set

A player (or players) who first wins six games wins a set, except that he must win by a margin of at least two games over his opponent, and where necessary a set shall be extended until this margin be achieved.

RULE 26

When Players Change Sides

The players shall change sides at the end of the first, third and every subsequent alternate game of each set, and at the end of each set unless the total number of games in such set be even, in which case the change is not made until the end of the first game of the next set.

RULE 27

Maximum Number of Sets

The maximum number of sets in a match shall be 5, or, where women take part, 3.

RULE 28

Rules Apply to Both Sexes

Except where otherwise stated, every reference in these Rules to the masculine includes the feminine gender.

RULE 29

Decisions of Umpire and Referee

In matches where an umpire is appointed, his decision

shall be final; but where a referee is appointed, an appeal shall lie to him from the decision of an umpire on a question of law, and in all such cases the decision of the referee shall be final.

The referee, at his discretion, may at any time postpone a match on account of darkness or the condition of the ground or the weather. In any case of postponement, the previous score and the previous occupancy of courts shall hold good, unless the referee and the players unanimously agree otherwise.

RULE 30

Play shall be continuous from the first service until the match be concluded, provided that after the third set, or when women take part, the second set, either player is entitled to a rest, which shall not exceed 10 minutes, or in countries situated between Latitude 15 degrees North and Latitude 15 degrees South, 45 minutes, and provided further that when necessitated by circumstances not within the control of the players, the umpire may suspend play for such a period as he may consider necessary. If play be suspended, and be not resumed until a later day, the rest may be taken only after the third set (or when women take part, the second set) of play on such later day, completion of an unfinished set being counted as one set. These provisions shall be strictly construed, and play shall never be suspended, delayed or interfered with for the purpose of enabling a player to recover his strength or his wind, or to receive instruction or advice. The umpire shall be the sole judge of such suspension, delay or interference, and after giving due warning he may disqualify the offender.

THE DOUBLES GAME

RULE 31

The above rules shall apply to the doubles game except as below.

RULE 32

Dimensions of Court

For the doubles game, the court shall be 36 feet in width, i.e., $4\frac{1}{2}$ feet wider on each side than the court for the singles game, and those portions of the singles sidelines which lie between the two service lines shall be called the service sidelines. In other respects, the court shall be similar to that described in Rule 1, but the portions of the singles sidelines between the baseline and service line on each side of the net may be omitted if desired.

RULE 33

Order of Service

The order of serving shall be decided at the beginning of each set as follows:

The pair who have to serve in the first game of each set shall decide which partner shall do so, and the opposing pair shall decide similarly for the second game. The partner of the player who served in the first game shall serve in the third; the partner of the player who served in the second game shall serve in the fourth, and so on in the same order in all the subsequent games of a set.

RULE 34

Order of Receiving

The order of receiving the service shall be decided at the beginning of each set as follows:

The pair who have to receive the service in the first game shall decide which partner shall receive the first service, and that partner shall continue to receive the first service in every odd game throughout that set. The opposing pair shall likewise decide which partner shall receive the first service in the second game, and that partner shall continue to receive the first service in every even game throughout that set. Partners shall receive the service alternately throughout each game.

RULE 35

Service Out of Turn

If a partner serve out of turn, the partner who ought to have served shall serve as soon as the mistake is discovered, but all points scored, and any faults served before such discovery, shall be reckoned. If a game shall have been completed before such discovery, the order of service remains as altered.

RULE 36

Error in Order of Receiving

If during a game the order of receiving the service is changed by the receivers, it shall remain as altered until the end of the game in which the mistake is discovered, but the partners shall resume their original order of receiving in the next game of that set in which they are receivers of the service.

121

RULE 37

Ball Touching Server's Partner is Fault

The service is a fault as provided for by Rule 9, or if the ball served touch the server's partner or anything he wears or carries, but if the ball served touch the partner of the receiver or anything which he wears or carries, not being a let under Rule 13 (a), before it hits the ground, the server wins the point.

RULE 38

Ball Struck Alternately

The ball shall be struck alternately by one or the other player of the opposing pairs, and if a player touches the ball in play with his racket in contravention of this Rule, his opponents win the point.